New Natives

New Natives

Becoming Indigenous in a Time of Crisis & Transition

Thomas Rain Crowe

Photographs by Simone Lipscomb

Iris Press
Oak Ridge, Tennessee

Copyright © 2025 by Thomas Rain Crowe

All rights reserved. No portion of this book may be reproduced in any form or by any means, including electronic storage and retrieval systems, without explicit, prior written permission of the publisher, except for brief passages excerpted for review and critical purposes.

ISBN: 978-1-60454-271-4

Some of these essays and poems appeared originally in *Crack Light* (Wind Publications), *The End of Eden* (Wind Publications) and the *Smoky Mountain News*. Text from "New Native" reprinted from *Zora's Field: My Life in the Appalachian Woods* (© 2005 by Thomas Rain Crowe) by permission of the University of Georgia Press.

Photographs Copyright © 2025 by Simone Lipscomb

Book Design: Robert B. Cumming, Jr.

Iris Press
www.irisbooks.com

Contents

Author's Note	11
Photographer's Note	19

Part I

Beauty	23
In Praise of Wilderness	27
The Spirit in Place	33
The Sacred	39
New Native	41
Native Tongue	51
The New Naturalists	55
A House in the Valley	63
The Wild Work	67
A Saint Among Us	73

Part II

The Aristocracy of the Wild	79
Walking the Woods	81
The Idiot's Wind	82
What *Is* Is	85
What Words Are Worth	87
Evensong	89
a beatnik wanders into Appalachia and learns the language of earth and sky	91
Mingus Mill	93
William Bartram Goes Hiking in the Wilderness And Falls in Love With a Beautiful Girl	95
The Names	97
No More Nationalism	99
Fall in Big Cataloochee Valley	101
The Change	103
May It Continue	104
Prayer For the Earth	107
Image Index	108

To be alive in this beautiful, self-organizing universe—to participate in the dance of life with senses to perceive it, lungs that breathe it, organs that draw nourishment from it—is a wonder beyond words.

—Joanna Macy

Author's Note

My concerns? In a word: the environment.
We're losing it to our insatiable hunger for consumption and commodities (things, stuff) and in our incompetence to manage and balance population and pollution in relation to what we think of as "growth" and "progress." Almost all of my work (writing and activism) these days has some foundation in my concern for the environment and what we have done to it and what **must** be done to stop the destruction and desecration of the planet and the atmosphere that surrounds it. This is critical and we **all** need to be working on this in one way or another—to try and put things back in a state of homeostasis.

I consider myself an independent person—someone who has "followed their bliss," as Joseph Campbell put it. "Done my own thing," as we used to say back in the 1960s. And in my adulthood, I've been self-employed. Yet, everywhere I've lived, I've lived as part of a community. I didn't live in isolation.

Yes, we are individuals and have, if we are lucky, the freedom to roam and choose how and where we live. But even so, we don't live in a vacuum. We live among other people and wild critters and landscapes—whether we acknowledge it or not. And each one of those landscapes, those environments, those places, influences and affects where we go, what we do, and who we become.

In my case, this is certainly true. I am an amalgam of the places and people and natural habitats I've spent time in and with. You could say I have MCD—a multiple-community disorder. But I'd rather think of it as a multiple-community order, an MCO, as I feel within myself an ordered harmony and clarity that is the result of having had the experiences I've had along this road I call "this life." As I near the end of this journey—this "hero's journey," if I may quote Campbell again—and as I witness the predicaments humans have unleashed upon the world through our inattention to the natural world and our selfish preoccupation with fulfilling individual desires, I see that Barry Lopez was right: the only way we're going to return to any kind of survivable equilibrium or stasis is to build a new, untraveled road into our future.

And that road won't be a solo journey—it must be built and traveled by whole communities, large and small. It's going to take a universal leap in consciousness, as eco-theologian Thomas Berry said—a group effort to allow us Homo sapiens to have any kind of future here on this garden planet we were so graciously given, called Earth.

In the biblical Gospel of Thomas, there is a passage that reads: "If you bring forth what is within you, what you bring forth will save you. If you do not bring forth what is within you, what you do not bring forth will destroy you." For the past several hundred years (or more), we humans have been following a paved path—one determined by nation-states, corporations, and

authoritarian governments, in the name of "progress"—to our own detriment. We've not been listening to the wisdom within, to the moral story within. That ignorance is now rising up to destroy us.

Barry Lopez, the Oregon-based naturalist writer, says we must think of our predicament not as a "problem," but as a metaphor. "You have to find a metaphor, and when you feel the surge of life, you're in the right place. We need to reinvent ourselves and our responsibilities to each other, our families, our communities, our countries, and our planet." He goes on: "If we're going to survive and to thrive in whatever landscape the world offers us in the decades ahead, we must learn to speak respectfully to each other, to listen to each other, to take into consideration the fate of each other's children. We need to wake up—wake up and become awoken to the salvation of a multicultural existence."

When Barry Lopez was traveling widely across the Arctic in the 1970s and '80s, he spent a lot of time among Inuit communities, and in each village he would ask people there what adjective they would use to describe white North American culture. The word he heard repeatedly was *lonely*. "They see us as deeply lonely people," he said, "and one of the reasons we're lonely is that we've cut ourselves off from the nonhuman world and have called this 'progress.' Such numinous encounters in nature are moments of reconnection, part of the human search for reciprocated love."

He further reflects upon this idea and these sentiments. "In my travels to different parts of the world, to Australia where I've traveled with Aboriginal people on their lands, in the Canadian High Arctic where I have traveled with the Inuit, I have been repeatedly struck by the same thought: if we are coming into a time of extreme environmental stress, recurring pandemics and of extreme social tensions, why is it that so few people who have actually dealt with these problems are not invited to the table for the discussion? We know why. Here are the questions of race, of cultural superiority, of patriarchy, of educational bias, of religious conviction, that cripple us when our effort is simply to care for our families, our progeny."

We need to take into consideration the customs and cultural wisdom of Native American wisdom-keepers on the subject. Onondaga, Iroquois elder Oren Lyons says that "our knowledge is profound and comes from living in one place for untold generations. It comes from watching the sun rise in the east and set in the west from the same place over great sections of time. We are as familiar with the lands, rivers, and great seas that surround us as we are with the faces of our mothers. Indeed, we call the earth Etenoba, our mother, from whence all life springs." His words are further mirrored by former Principal Chief of the Cherokee Nation Wilma Mankiller when she writes in her autobiography, "Cooperation has always been necessary for the survival of tribal people. And even today, working together is more conducive to success

than competing with one another." In support of Wilma Mankiller's wisdom as a legendary leader of her people the Oklahoman newspaper wrote of her: "Wilma Mankiller, the first Principal Chief of the Cherokee Nation, helped all Americans understand the need to preserve the basic value of community and stewardship which are central to Native American culture. Above all, through her example she taught us the power of kindness and how to live and die with dignity." We can also cite primary passages from Robin Wall Kimmerer's recent non-fiction best-seller *Braiding Sweetgrass* for focus and references on "community" and interaction among the plants and animals in the natural world. She gives particular attention to maple trees and how they communicate. Also, she stresses the importance of communication with tribal peoples and the natural world. Finally, none other than feminist, activist and author Gloria Steinem writes: "Native American tribal life through the centuries was far from a primitive way of life. Inner space was as explored by the many as outer space is now explored by the few. The ways of nature and animals, of creating language and art, of healing illness and preserving food, of governing and resolving conflicts had already been perfected over millennia."

Specifically, and maybe more to the eco-psychological point, in his latest novel Henry Mitchell writes in *The Winged Child:*

> Plants get along much better than people do. They have to, because what we strive for individually, they can only attain in community. Plants know as much as we do, maybe a lot more. They just have their own ways of knowing it. We could learn a lot from them if we could speak the same language. Trees are more connected with their universe than we are. They are not burdened with ego and intellectual constructs. They are not blinded by self-observation. They simply participate in any definable life form, as in the sum of its connections with other life forms.

He goes on to say that we have to:

> know how to listen apart from words, deeper than emotion, calmer than logic. How to still beneath the storm of rational, linear analysis, to rest in the harmony embedded in all contradiction, to fall into deep awareness of the other until there is no longer any I and Thous, only We. What one thinks of as oneself as just the surface of the life that is there. Knowing, awareness, intention, run deep. Deeper than we can see. Deeper than we can imagine. Deeper than unto ourselves alone, we are.

Our contemporary wisdom-keepers are everywhere if we are open and attuned to them and are striving to help us to not only know ourselves, but to learn how to live together and in harmony with our identified natural and human communities.

Kairos is an ancient Greek word meaning "the right, critical, or opportune moment." It is one of two words that the ancient Greeks had for "time;" the other being *chronos*. Whereas the latter refers to chronological or sequential time, *kairos* signifies a proper or opportune time for action. It is now a term

being widely used by social scientists and environmental physicists to address the conditions in which we find ourselves living today. In other words, *Now* is the proper time for action—in this opportune moment when we are told by everyone in the know that if we are going to have a sustainable world in which to live we must make the necessary changes both to ourselves and to everyone around us.

Or as Thomas Berry indicates:

> The historic mission of our times is to reinvent the human—at the species level, with critical reflection, within the community of life systems, in a time-developmental context, by means of story, and shared dream experience. We must invent, or reinvent, a sustainable human culture by a descent into our pre-rational, our instinctive resources. Our cultural resources have lost their integrity. They cannot be trusted. What is needed is not transcendence but 'inscendence,' not the brain but the gene.

In other words, we are going to need to, as the Beatles song implies, "Come Together." A song that rings out today with its more than pertinent title and urgent message: "Come together, right now." We must "come together" with reciprocated love as Lopez names it, and with "now" meaning today—there is no time to waste!

—Thomas Rain Crowe

Photographer's Note

John Seed once said, "I am part of the rain forest protecting itself." The idea he shares is that we are One with all life, and when we are open, we can take action as an extension of the Earth protecting itself.

I first learned of John Seed when I spent a week with Joanna Macy and thirty other individuals learning about Deep Ecology and healing our disconnect from Earth. This was after I spent a year documenting the BP Deepwater Horizon Gulf of Mexico oil spill disaster. I was emotionally and spiritually burned out, depressed, exhausted. Joanna helped me heal and open myself again to align with beauty.

Twenty-five years after the explosion of Deepwater Horizon—an event that killed eleven workers and created the largest oil spill in the history of marine oil drilling operations—I was hiking with friends on Alum Cave trail. We made it to LeConte Lodge and enjoyed lunch. One friend decided to stay at the lodge and rest, so another friend and I decided to hike to Cliff Tops, a short distance from the lodge.

There are two trails to Cliff Tops, and I led us up the longer one. As soon as we turned onto Cliff Tops trail, off of the Boulevard Trail, we smelled smoke and saw a billowing puff coming from a grassy area. Without looking at each other to talk about it or pausing, we sprinted through the woods toward the smoke and found an actively burning fire in a very poorly constructed circle of rocks. Dry grass surrounded the site, and high winds were blowing.

My friend Paige, a battalion chief in a fire department in Georgia, immediately took action. She worked on suppressing the fire, and I ran for more water and to alert the lodge staff. The fire was quickly extinguished, and a potential catastrophe averted.

Never have I felt like two individuals were so in the right place at the right time. The wind was blowing toward the lodge. One spark blown from the strong winds could have created a loss of historic structures, forest, wildlife, and even human life. The experience reminded me of John Seed's quote: "I am part of the rainforest protecting itself."

Perhaps our openness to Nature—to service—allowed the forest to rise up through us to protect itself. Our love of Nature called us to that intersection of need and skill.

Imagine what could happen in our lives—and in this world—if many of us were open to using our skills and allowed life to call us to the sacred intersections where need and skill meet. Not just once, but as a life practice. I believe the world could be transformed.

—Simone Lipscomb

Part I

Beauty

Usually an early riser, these days I find I'm getting up later—8:00, 8:30, 9:00, 9:30. It's as if my subconscious is resisting, not wanting to face the day. I'm usually a hopeful person—searching the darkness for a sign of light. These days, however, my mood is much more often one of resignation. I find that I'm walking about in the world looking for signs of natural beauty while I still can, unsure of how much longer it (Nature) or we (the human species) will be around to enjoy it.

Flooding. Hurricanes. Earthquakes. Tornadoes. Tsunamis. Drought. Global warming. In addition to all the weather news, there are stories of pandemics, greedy politicians, oil mongers, corporate raiders and mindless terrorism. I'm reminded of a true story I heard about twenty-five years ago told by a renown Sufi teacher—about a meeting that he had had with his guru. When visiting India during the early 1960s at the height of nuclear escalation and conflict between Russia and the United States, and sitting at the feet of this wise and gray-bearded man, he asked the question: "What is going to happen to us, to everything?" After a long pause the elderly prophet turned to the young Sufi novitiate and said, "It's not what you think." "Do you mean that there is not going to be a nuclear war or some sort of nuclear holocaust," the younger man responded. Again there was a long puase, until finally the old man looked the younger in the eye and said, "Mass insanity."

This story, to me, seems to sum up and explain almost everything we're experiencing today. Moderation has been thrown out with both the baby and the bathwater. Everything man-made is being conceived and done in excess. It's as if the Earth woke up one day this year, took a look around, and shouted, "I'm mad as hell, and I'm not going to take it anymore!"

The "end of the world" cartoons that appear regularly in the printed media are beginning to look more and more pragmatic—prophetic. If one looks at the data offered up by the scientific community—regarding economics, ozone and CO_2 pollution, population, and so on—the arc of all graphs converge around the year 2000 and shoot straight up, skyward, out of sight. In the past two hundred years—following what had previously been millennia of relative environmental stability—instability in the environment has steadily been on the rise, and what we're looking at, now and into the indefinite future, is a dubious lifestyle based on essential maintenance and repair. In fact, what we may be witnessing is the end of Eden.

At a talk given to the Environmental Leadership Council at Warren Wilson College, ninety-one year old ecologian (a title designed especially for him combining the fields of ecology and theology), Thomas Berry told his audience, "We're looking at a new era in Earth history. I call it The Ecozoic period. Ecology will dominate both the news and our consciousness. With combined planetary periods ever-present, we're looking at a new paradigm for humanity. This will mean a new era of activism that will fall predominatly on the shoulders of the younger generation, who will inherit the dubious job of recovery and reinhabitation of our natural habitat—saving what's left of Eden—manning the social programs that will care for the unexpectedly displaced and destitute at a time when food, health and shelter can no longer be taken for granted."

With a similar message given to an all-too-sparse audience at Western Carolina University in Cullowhee, noted scientist and expert on global climate change William Schlesinger said, "The rising human population, currently at 6.5 billion, has brought about changes in the basic chemistry of earth's atmosphere and oceans, which have formed the evolutionary environment for all life now on Earth. There has been irreparable damage. The Arctic ice we are losing, for example, will never be replaced. To ignore climate change and other global environmental problems is fundamentally and ethically wrong."

With experts like these lined up in agreement, the writing is on the wall. The garden-world of the planet Earth is fast disappearing, and being replaced by a noxious environment created from man's disrespect for Nature and his greed for material and personal wealth and would-be comfort. The end of Eden.

In essence, what I've said above is: that there is a need for serious discussion of taboo topics, such as overpopulation, global warming, free-trade capitalism. These are the true issues that are at the heart of what's wrong in the world. Everything else is just a symptom of these greater "illnesses."

Until recently, I never really believed in the idea of "evil." But these days, given the behavior of the mega-corporations and certain people in government in both the statehouse in Raleigh, NC and in Washington DC, I'm beginning to rethink my previous position. What I used to see as misguided and uninformed behavior, more and more, seems to be down-right destructive, and yes, even evil.

In bleak times like these in which we are living, what, then, can we do? To that imposing question, all I can do is to share with you the epiphany I had the other night while eating supper and listening to the evening news. In the midst of a string of depressing stories on the Middle East, global warming, the privatization of public lands, and corporate raiding, a single thought came to me: Flood the collective human consciousness and senses with all the beauty we can muster! Music, voice, language, literature, architecture, art, advertising, product design... Everything seen and heard. The shadow world of ignorance and greed, while a powerful one, has no defense against beauty. Of this I am convinced.

We don't need to fight fire with fire, or respond in kind to the ways of the wicked and the monetarily possessed. If we just flood the marketplaces, the pages of our papers, the air waves, the museums, the theatres, the shops, the streets, our computer and our minds with beauty, I believe we'll have a chance to turn things around. It's a subtle, if not radical approach. But it just may be worth a try.

While this may seem to some a little far-fetched, it's the best idea I've had lately. I believe, by flooding the streets, the marketplace, the pages of our papers, the airwaves, the museums, the theaters, the shops and our minds and language with beauty, we, too, can "tame" the more primitive and self-indulgent urges of the beast of progress and ownership. We can, in fact, turn things around.

Credit: *The End of Eden: Writings of an Environmental Activist,* Wind Publications, 2008.

In Praise of Wilderness

I was lucky enough to have been involved in the foundational days of the Bioregional Movement on the west coast during the 1970s. I was working with and around people like Peter Berg of *Planet Drum*, Lee Swenson of *Simple Living*, poet Gary Snyder, and others. What I learned from these poets and provacateurs was that *biodiversity* is the sustaining reality throughout all of nature. It is, in the end, diversity which allows for the quality of life of all living things, as well as allowing everything to survive and to evolve, and to continue. Once the idea or the reality of monocultures takes root, everything starts becoming like everything else around it—the gene pool is weakened, and the quality of life is compromised.

Diversity, for me, is essential in both philosophical and practical ways. It is essential to the natural world—meaning it's also essential to the human world. I think it's a wonderful thing that we have different geographical bioregions, different cultures, and different peoples, different races, different languages, different religions and belief systems. Life would be fairly dull, don't you think, if we were all the same color and there was only one variety of tree, and one kind of salamander, and one way to think of or worship God? In this kind of mono-world, our imaginations, which are essentially fueled by the natural world and the diversity and mystery of the Universe, would go flat, dry. Entropy would set in. We would cease to be the creative creatures we are. Having had my eyes opened to this paradigm, and believing that diversity is necessary for the well-being of all living creatures and systems, it is easy for me to say, now, and with conviction, that I am not willing to live in a world absent of elephants and whales!

Pulitzer Prize-winning biologist E.O. Wilson in his book *Half-Earth: Our Planet's Fight for Life* discusses the premise that a huge variety of life-forms on Earth still remain largely unknown to science and that the species discovered and studied well enough to assess, notably the vertebrae animals and flowering plants, are declining in number at an accelerating rate—due almost entirely to human activity. In response to this premise, Wilson very succinctly states: "The global conservation movement has temporarily mitigated but hardly stopped the on-going extinction of species. The rate of loss is instead accelerating. If biodiversity is to be returned to the baseline level of extinction of inviolable numbers that existed before the spread of humanity, and thus saved for future generations, the conservation effort must be raised to a new level. The only solution to the "Sixth Extinction" is to increase the area of inviolable natural reserves to half the surface of the Earth or greater. But it also requires a fundamental shift in moral reasoning concerning our relation to the living environment."

The hook-line phrase in the above paragraph is "increase the area of inviolable natural reserves (i.e. Wilderness designated land reserves) to *half* the surface of the Earth," hence echoing the book's title. Half of our planet saved as Wilderness or wild lands seems an awful lot given the shrinking size of the planet due to global markets, global population statistics and the Internet and social media. But after reading Wilson's compilation of facts and figures and prescient logic, one can only agree with his compassionate analysis and fears for the future of all species, including humans. His omniscient observations and study of species extinction hit hard and very close to home as he cites our own Great Smoky Mountains National Park as his primary referent example. Wilson says:

> It is instructive to proceed to the Great Smoky Mountains National Park, one of the best-studied American reserves, and to reflect briefly on the breakdown of the numbers of known species in each group of organisms. The actual number of recorded species in the Park, especially when all suspected but still unrecorded transient species and microorganisms are added, has been estimated to lie between sixty thousand and eighty thousand.

Very impressive numbers, these, and those living in these western North Carolina mountains are immensely fortunate to be living in such a diverse neighborhood. Yet, we should be humbled by such numbers, or as Wilson goes on to say:

> The wildlands and the bulk of Earth's biodiversity protected within them are another world from the one humanity is throwing together pell-mell. What do we receive from them? The stabilization of the global environment they provide and their very existence are the gifts they give to us. We are their stewards, not their owners. These wildlands of the world are not art museums. They are not gardens to be arranged and tended for our delectation. They are not recreation centers or harborers of natural resources or sanatoriums or undeveloped sites of business opportunities.

Wilson's layman-friendly book is full of scientific evidence to support his predictions as well as his solutions to this very real and urgent global crisis we all seem to be ignoring, at our own peril.

Wilson is not alone with his convincing data and his dire predictions. Many esteemed scientists, economists, social scientists, artists and politicians world-wide agree with Wilson's findings and predictions. Or as Wilson says in his ending chapter ("The Solution"):

> The pivotal conclusion to be drawn remains forever the same: by destroying most of the biosphere with archaic short-term methods, we are setting ourselves up for a self-inflicted disaster. Across eons the diversity of species has created ecosystems that provide a maximum level of stability.

Climate changes and uncontrollable catastrophes from earthquakes, volcanic eruptions, and asteroid strikes have thrown nature off balance, but in relatively short geologic periods of time, the damage was repaired—due to the great variety and resilience of the life-forms on Earth.

Here in the Southern Appalachians and elsewhere, Earth's shield of biodiversity is being shattered and the pieces are being thrown away. In its place is being inserted only the promise that all can be solved by human ingenuity. Some hope that we can take over the controls, monitor the sensors, and push the right buttons to run Earth the way we choose. In response, all the rest of us should be asking: Can the planet be run as a true spaceship by one intelligent species? Surely we would be foolish to take such a large and dangerous gamble. Or as Wilson says:

> There is nothing our scientists and political leaders can do to replace the still unimaginable complex of niches and the interactions of the millions of species that fill them. If they try, as some of them seem determined to do, and then even if they succeed to some extent, remember we won't be able to go back. The result will be irreversible.

We have only one planet, one mountain chain known as the Appalachians, and we are allowed only one such experiment. These all depend upon the balance that is created by a diverse biosphere. Diversity is not only preferable, it is paramount. Why make a world-threatening and unnecessary gamble by continuing in the direction that the human race is going in if a safe option is open? E.O. Wilson's option is for humans to relinquish control and ownership and to surrender enough additional land into wilderness to total one half the surface of the Earth. You get what you give up.

The Spirit in Place

...before the coming of Christianity all the peoples of the Old World had lived in a numinous landscape spangled with sacred markers and sacred places. The land itself was believed to be alive and under the protection of numina, guardian spirits. In such a world one did not blithely cut down a grove of trees, plow up virgin meadowland, dam a stream or divert it. An alteration of the landscape had to be carefully couched in a propitiatory ritual. Intended to appease the numina.

—Frederick Turner
Spirit of Place: The Making of an American Landscape

In the 1980s, while working as director of a project to identify and protect Native American sacred sites in the Southern Appalachians, my partners and I faced considerable opposition from big landowners, real estate developers, and self-serving local government officials. This took the form of everything from slanderous attacks and character assassinations in local and regional newspapers to, in one case, death threats. My loosely knit team of traditional Cherokee elders, folklorists, archaeologists, and volunteers—both Native American and Anglo—were fighting what was clearly an uphill battle, if not an escalating war. But we persisted—at least long enough to see sanctions written into the National Forest Service's "50-Year Plan," which included mandatory consultation with Cherokee officials before logging or building roads on Forest Service land. These regulations were designed to safeguard and protect areas slated for logging that might include sites of religious or historical importance.

During these years, we experienced a kind of revival regarding white, European interest in "native" matters—particularly in the ethnological heritage of the people in this region. Here in western North Carolina, as soon as it became okay—or "cool"—to admit to Indian bloodlines in their family lineage, I began receiving phone calls, letters, and faxes almost daily. People asked about places that might have religious or historical significance in their area or on their land. Others inquired about how to get in-depth genealogical counseling.

All kinds of questions. All kinds of stories and family histories.

We had, quite literally, opened a genealogical and cultural Pandora's box. While there was, on one hand, a battle going on between the project directors and the powers that be, there was also, simultaneously, a sort of ethnological renaissance occurring throughout the broader western North Carolina population. It seemed that a long-held denial was beginning to give way to acceptance. Interest was replacing apathy.

Today, following a major blood-degree controversy, the ousting of a principal chief on grounds of corruption, the emergence of a strong traditional activist movement, and the building of the Harrah's Cherokee Casino, things are very different on the Qualla Boundary. For the first time in what some would say has been a very long time, there are many more visible and public signs that traditional life is alive and well.

During the reign of Robert Youngdeer as principal chief, the tribe's official stance on traditional practices was, "The Cherokee no longer practice the old traditional ways." And yet, during this time, the tribe recognized traditional elders such as Walker Calhoun and Jerry Wolfe. A reinvigorated Cherokee Language Program was also promoted by the Tribal Council, focusing on the youngest tribal members in an effort to keep the language and traditional culture from extinction. Old dances, songs, and cultural consciousness are being preserved and shared through the public appearances and touring performances of the Warriors of Anikituhwa. The old ways are becoming part of the new ways, and a more appropriate balance is being reached. Understandings of what is sacred are evolving—as all things do and should.

At the same time, the dominant culture is also undergoing change, as population demographics in western North Carolina shift with the influx of first- and second-home residents. Many of these "new natives" bring with them ecological and ethnic values rooted in their previous environments. While the migration of second-home buyers and developers from urban areas has had some negative effects, the long-term influence of conservation-minded individuals has been largely positive. This is evidenced by the growth in number and strength of various environmental organizations throughout the region. With all the media coverage and controversy surrounding pressing environmental concerns here, the question of the sacredness of the natural world continues to arise—again and again.

North Carolina native and ecologian Thomas Berry wrote in his 1999 landmark publication *The Great Work*, "In the end, it is the land that is the most sacred element of our lives." This is not some kind of New Age or hippie heresy. To my mind, it's just plain common sense. If we don't hold the Earth and its life forms as sacred—as worthy of reverence and stewardship—then we are, in a very real way, jeopardizing our own welfare. Without a healthy environment, humans cannot live healthy lives. One thing determines the other. Without the essentials of clean air, fresh water, and fertile soil, all other systems are irrelevant.

Later, during the Sacred Sites Project, I witnessed not only traditional ceremonies but also spent time in sacred places that truly felt imbued with a numinous energy or a presiding divinity—a presence that was not only physically perceptible but also remarkable. I noticed a pattern: these places—waterfalls, groves of trees, springs, mountain peaks, rock cliffs—shared geographic characteristics. Encountering them during the course of everyday travel always gave me pause, causing me to slow down, pay attention, and take notice.

As I became more enamored with these "special" places, one of our project elders pulled me aside and gave me a talking-to.

"All places are sacred," he said. "All equally, and they should be treated as such. The idea that one place is more sacred than another is foreign to our Cherokee beliefs. Everything is sacred. To divide and separate one thing from another is a white man's concept. We believe that everything is interrelated and part of a larger web of life."

I often wonder what the implications of that kind of thinking are for all of us today. If we embrace such a worldview, then how can we respond with anything but horror to regional environmental travesties such as the toxification of the Barber Orchards Superfund site in Haywood County, the pollution of the Pigeon River by the former paper plant in Canton, the smog from coal-fired power plants around the Great Smoky Mountains, or the history of clear-cutting by the U.S. Forest Service?

And more broadly—how can we justify any human activity carried out in the natural world (including our towns and cities) that lacks reverence, respect, and regard for future generations?

What is sacred? In a very real sense—as Indigenous peoples have believed for millennia—the Earth itself is a sacred temple, a church, a gift and a covenant from the Creator. Or, as Kentucky poet Wendell Berry proclaims, "What I stand for / is what I stand on." Would we dare to swear inside a church—or desecrate it? If not, why should we be any less respectful toward the Earth, which literally sustains our lives?

When I am in my garden here beside the Tuckasegee River, I try to work with a sense of reverence—for the rich soil and the relatively clean water nearby. I grow my crops organically, without resorting to easy poisons. I do this out of respect for myself, for my family, and for the continued well-being of the land—so that others who come after me may also benefit. That they, too, may one day harvest healthy food from this place.

Many years have gone by, and I am now in my elder years. Only now am I truly beginning to replace my European values—with their emphasis on separation and isolation—with those of my traditional Cherokee neighbors, who view the world much more holistically.

I'm making progress. My Cherokee friends tease me. "You'll get it someday," they say, laughing.

And I know I still have a long way to go. But I'm working—diligently—to see the bigger picture that comes so easily to my Indigenous friends: a picture in which everything is connected, and *everything* is sacred.

The Sacred

The seed of spirit is in the flower.
And the flower lives in the garden of all things.

Nowhere has the rock or the wood
become so fertile as in the womb of the earth.
In the hands of plants.
And in the stormy dreams of the gods.

Like the farmer who tills sand along the shoreline of the sea
or poets without ink,
we are born into this world of grace.
With only the seeds of memory and a song
of our ancient race.

Through the warm tears of love
the eyes of fire in the mountains dance.
How quickly the mind becomes water
as we gaze at the moon!
This silver
that lays side by side with gold in the poem of night.
And like the dew, this moon will pass away.
EVERYTHING is sacred!

New Native

In a distinct, diverse and interdependent part of the planetary biosphere that deserves a unique social, political and cultural identity to match its natural endowment, it would be possible for us to deliberately put a renewed culture into harmony with the natural flows of energy and life—in a process that could be called reinhabitation. We can become natives.
—Peter Berg
Planet Drum Review, summer 1981

With rain coming down in snare-like drumbeats on the tin roof of my cabin, I'm holed up this afternoon inside. Sitting here in my sheepskin-lined nineteenth-century rocker held together with twine, grapevines, and Elmer's glue, reading Donald Culross Peattie's *Flowering Earth* and thinking deeply about the time I spent in Gary Snyder's community up along the San Juan Ridge north of Nevada City in the Sierra foothills. In his book Peattie writes: "For every man there is some spot on earth, I think, which he has pledged himself to return to, some day, because he was so happy there once." This has certainly been true in my case, for I remember the years of my youth in the Smokies as being not only informative but also very happy. And perhaps that same happiness accounts for why I am here now.

Most of the folks inhabiting the North San Juan Ridge in the Sierra Nevada mountains of California were living what we referred to as a "bio-regional lifestyle," largely manifested by escaping from the city, cultivating a small vegetable garden, participating in periodic season community ceremonies and rituals, and studying and partly adhering to Buddhist and Native American religious and social ideology and practice. In those days Gary had defined "bio-regionalism" as a reference to "the tiny number of persons who come out of the industrial societies and then start to turn back to the land, to place. This comes for some with the rational and scientific realization of interconnectedness, and planetary limits. But the actual demands of a life committed to a place, and living somewhat by the sunshine green plant energy that is concentrated in that spot, are so physically and intellectually intense, that it is moral and spiritual choice as well." This newborn bio-regional movement, in which I participated during the late 1970s, also included ideas of reinhabitation, ecological awareness, and giving constitutional-type rights to nonhuman species; and it was manifest in the establishment of the *Planet Drum Review,* the Reinhabitory Theatre, the Primitive Arts Institute, and the All Species Day Parade, as well as in the creation of an alternative school and an enthusiastic volunteer fire department. All these undertakings and much more were based on the belief that the well-being of the Earth depends upon our understanding the importance of biological diversity and correct relationship to place—place viewed in both its microcosmic and macro cosmic incarnations as it dovetails with our day-to-day lives and stewardship of the place we call home. It is here at home, I believe, that "the real work," as Gary Snyder calls it, begins. And that real work these days must begin with rediscovering and establishing intimacy with the natural world. In fact I would go so far as to say that only this kind of intimacy can save us from the current mega-maniacal plundering of the natural world—which we are clearly, consciously or unconsciously, carrying out, while at the same time causing the extinction of hundreds, if not thousands, of animal and plant species every year.

Most of us have come to live where we do as uninvited guests from other places, other cultures. Many, maybe most, of the people who have moved into the mountains of western North Carolina from the outside have come here oblivious to and unconcerned about what has culturally preceded them. Unaware of biology, geology, geography, genealogy, and the historical and cultural balances built into natural and social systems that have coexisted and cohabitated in relative harmony for untold generations prior to the arrival of the latest wave of incoming migrants.

By "new native" I mean those persons who have come to live in a place, either physically or mentally, for the first time and yet feel it is truly home. New natives are caretakers of the old as well as heralds of the new. They come into a place (in my case the mountains of western North Carolina, what some are calling the Katuah Bio-region after a village and spiritual center of the Cherokee nation) with a sense of reverence and responsibility, recognizing that it is their inherent duty to respect the past, enjoy the present, and safeguard the future.

I returned home to these Smoky Mountains—after a sojourn away that lasted almost twenty years—to embark upon a life of relative isolation and self-sufficiency. My world here in Zoro's field is very different from the world on the other side of these woods, with its shopping malls, its computers, its consumer-driven media, its TV … Despite my attempts at monkishness and anonymity, word of my Thoreau-like lifestyle here in the Green River woodlands has leaked out beyond the protective borders of trees and water. Recently I have been approached by outsiders to become involved in activities and organizations—such as a project to identify and protect Native American sacred sites in the southern Appalachians and to help create a bio-regional journal in the Southeast. All this attention is attributable, I assume, to my farming experience, as well as to my current wilderness lifestyle coming on the heels of my former life with the Planet Drum folks on the West Coast.

So I guess my roving and ruckus-raising over the years has proven to be useful in that it has allowed me to bring home some of the goods and the good news acquired in the process. Whether or not I'll become deeply involved

in these projects remains to be seen—as I am reluctant to compromise the pristine nature of my privacy and risk the schizophrenia of living here while trying to work with people on the outside with their "civilized" values and notions. Maybe I can figure out a way to work from my "bee-loud glade" as a consultant, not having to partake of life amidst the maddening crowds. At the same time, because of my West Coast experience, I feel obligated to do my part in spreading the word.

To my way of thinking, and at the core of the ideals of the new native, there is an understanding that what the modern world has given us, has offered up as "progress," is not healthy, healing, meaningful, or good for either individual or planet, and that the patriarchy and the subterfuge-aggressiveness manifested in the accumulation of wealth and power (and further manifested as the psychosis that leads to nationalism and constant war) will fall back eventually, like sand, into the sea of a repetitive and fruitless history. In my experience both on the West Coast and in Zoro's field, when living with the mind-set and focus of reinhabitation it becomes possible for realities such as extended family, for instance, to reestablish themselves as part of our living culture. It becomes possible for clans and stewardship communities to be started or revived and then to survive within the framework of sustainable local economies based on meaningful work and social structures that are, in turn, based on fraternal intercourse rather than on economic, racial, and religious feuding. The new native ideal advocates an even more finely tuned sensitivity to reinhabitation, incorporating not only the notion of the collective unconscious but a transfiguration of one's psyche into a more spiritual and sense-liberated whole. Hypothetically, it produces total beings whose values and sociosexual politics are more in harmony with the psychosexual balance of watershed-ecosystem and with the planet and the universe.

While the role models for my reinhabitory life in the Green River watershed are the myriad species of animals that have lived, ranged, and procreated here for millennia, our true cultural ancestors and exemplars for living with a sense of place here in western North Carolina (and in North America generally) are the American Indians. Even at this late juncture, I don't think it's preposterous to suggest that we of European descent still owe a rather large karmic debt for our genocidal relationship with the original human inhabitants of this continent. With respect to this would-be debt, I think a good place to begin resolution and settlement would be through bio-centered, region-centered education and, further, through the incorporation of the knowledge, sensibilities, and traditional wisdom of these peoples into our own consciousness, culture, and lifestyle.

I am not advocating that we become carbon copies of the Native Americans of the past. Being a new native entails, rather, embracing, without guilt, a consciousness that learns from the cultures that have been

here longest and therefore know the place best. With this education and awareness gained, new rituals, celebrations, and lifestyles may be conceived and carried out, compatible with the past but reflections of an ongoing sustainable present. The next step will be redefining and re-inhabiting the place in which we live and thereby becoming truly modern. Not modern in a postindustrial sense, but modern in reference to the creative ways we manifest new designs of living that make us participants with rather than competitors against the natural world. These thoughts are echoed for me in lines from Ruth Beebe Hill's book *Hanta Yo:*

But the truly wonderful things, the great mysteries, move quietly.
Who will hear the sun climb the sky, hear the grasses push up?

Indeed, who will be the visionaries, the mythic ministers, of our Postindustrial period (what Thomas Berry calls the Ecozoic Era)? The quiet ones who are living at the pace of nature, at the speed of life, who can hear the sun climbing the sky, the grass pushing up through decaying leaves in the spring? Will there even be a wilderness in that future? And who, if any of us, will live in it? And how? Thomas Berry is full of profound thoughts on the future of humanity in the natural world. "In the end," he says, "it is the land that is the most sacred element of our lives." To my way of thinking, if we don't hold the earth and all its life as sacred and worthy of reverence, we are undermining our own well-being. Without a healthy, mentally balanced life. One thing predetermines the other. Without breathable air and potable water where would we be? Without a diverse and expansive range of plants and animals where would we be? Without the flowers and bees, the pine nuts and squirrels, the berries and bears . . . where would we be? Where will we be when all this is altered, compromised, or gone? I, for one, am clear about this idea of diversity and my relationship with other species. I don't want to live in a world absent of elephants and whales.

Community

"I am a storyteller, and I think stories communicate. When a community starts to get a story, it becomes a community. People are freaking out because they can't fit themselves into a local story, or into any story. If you don't have one you have to make it up, and if there is no local culture, you have to make it," says Gurney Norman in Simple Living magazine in the fall of 1976. Thinking about Norman's quote and possible futures for humankind calls up my own past. I can remember how isolated it felt growing up as a boy in the deep mountains of Graham County. Winters tended to be more severe than they are today, and there were sometimes long stretches when folks couldn't get in or out of the little town of Robbinsville, which intensified the kind of tribal feeling that occurred during bad weather. The community ethos was a warm one, and I remember feeling secure, knowing that in hard times we could take care of one another and that life somehow would continue as it always had.

Those were formative years for me. Years that instilled in me an idealistic picture of community and at the same time gave me a strong sense of independence and self. These memories include the congregation of great groups of kids at elder persons' homes to crack burlap pokes (sacks) full of walnuts, and neighborhood workdays to help someone pick tobacco or to build or repair barns. It's true I was just a boy and so hadn't experienced the kinds of antagonistic things that adults can do to each other, breaking or at least disturbing community relations, but the idea and experience of community I enjoyed as a boy has stayed with me through the years.

As they say, those were the good old days, and those days and those kinds of sentiments have faded. Even in small towns like Saluda here in rural Polk County the word "community" is rarely used. Old buildings that have served as community centers and general stores outside of the town proper are used rarely and are often in disrepair. Almost all the roads have been paved and are busy with continuous traffic night and day. These days one is more likely to catch up on news and local gossip in the housewares sections of the new superstores near Asheville than at a community center potluck or from friends casually dropping in—as they used to do with regularity in former times. The American Heritage Dictionary of the English Language defines "community" as "a group of plants and animals living in a specific region under relatively similar conditions; ecology; fellowship." This is a good place to start, as the idea of community, according to this definition, encompasses not only human life but plants and animals also—and the term "ecology" helps put things in a more complete and proper perspective. Not only are intercourse and interaction implied but also stewardship and education—both of which in the old days might have been considered essential to the well-being of the community. And let's not forget the fellowship that in those days was a regular and continuous conversation among those whose paths would cross in the barbershop, the feed store, or the general store as the years and generations passed . . . These days we barely know our neighbors and are more likely to spend extensive time with TV sitcom families than with our own. Times have changed, and in my more insecure moments I find that I miss the old days of my boyhood in the Milltown neighborhood of Robbinsville along Snowbird Creek—the naive innocence, the prepubescent camaraderie, the woods and the creeks as places to play.

"Most important," the Kentucky poet and farmer Wendell Berry writes, "a community must be generally loved and competently cared for by its people, who, individually, identify their own interest with the interest of their neighbors. This notion of community began to vanish in America after World War II. Our small towns have never been worse off than they are now." Everywhere I look on the subject of community, I find references to fellowship and sustainable economy.

Among his writings on global cultures and ecology, Thomas Berry (no relation to Wendell Berry) has written this on the subject of community: "We have lost immense areas of intimate knowledge carried in traditional craft and in farming skills, knowledge that provides a relationship between the human community and the natural world that is immensely more bountiful and less destructive than that of large-scale business projects." As our communities have broken down and been replaced with sundry technologies and corporations, the skills that fostered neighborliness have been lost in a single generation.

Today community has more to do with consumerism than with conservation and commonality. And with regard to the ecology side of the coin Thomas Berry adds: "The well-being of each component part [of the community] is intimately related to the well-being of the other parts and to the well-being of the whole."

I have been taken aback by this solitary and monkish thinker Thomas Berry. My notebooks are filled with his words. An apostle of the great French eco-philosopher Pierre Teilhard de Chardin, Berry has carried the torch of planetary and personal wisdom further up the mountain of enlightenment and leadership. From my notebook I read: "Every mode of being has inherent rights to their place in the single community that is the Earth community, rights that come by existence itself. The intimacy of humans with the other components of the planet is the fulfillment of each in the other and all within the single Earth community. It is a spiritual fulfillment as well as a mutual support. It is a commitment, not simply a way of survival."

Living in the woods I am beginning to understand these words. My community includes as much (and maybe more) the plant and animal life as it does the human. Living as we do in proximity with each other, it is necessary that we live harmoniously and with mutual respect. And in terms of interdependence, I see clearly that the plants and animals are far less dependent upon me than I upon them. It is no accident that almost all creation stories and myths of indigenous peoples on this and other continents include animals and plants at their origin, in some cases humans being derivative of one or another animal species. Early peoples saw how inextricable human life is from the natural world. This can be seen most dramatically, perhaps, in the fact that people were often given the names of animals and plants, and they bore them with honor. Humans once knew the importance of interdependence and cohabitation with the plant and animal kingdoms. Today with industry and technology removing us further and further from our former relationships with the natural world, we take our animal neighbors for granted at best, and we slaughter them into extinction at worst.

While I don't live a town life anymore, and much prefer my own company or that of my animal friends to human social gatherings, I still think with compassion of the vast majority of people who cannot escape constant human interaction and conflict. I have read some of the new future-primitive prophets who speak of a rural future for the planet, predicting that we are entering an era when small towns will be valued again and that out of necessity we will reinvent social economies using local assets and resources. While this kind of talk is inviting, it seems foolish to think that humanity will, at this late date, literally go back to the "good old days." However, we may in increments be able to move forward to the "good new ways"—which might include essential and traditional aspects of the old, such as embracing the reinhabitory idea of community. Communities that operate with greater degrees of social, cultural, and governmental autonomy and where currencies are circulated and recycled—filtering money back into local receptacles to benefit those who have come upon hard times and been forced to live on less. These new communities, as I envision them, would be based on the self-realized merits of each of their members, where every person has a place and finds appropriate and meaningful work. In this paradigm, work is generated, barter is encouraged, and community members do not have to leave home in order to survive, as they often do in the rural communities of western North Carolina today. Community becomes a place of "continuous harmony," as Wendell Berry has called it, a place that functions simply and therefore well.

Thinking on this I am reminded of Occam's Razor, an axiom that proposes that the simplest and most direct way to do anything is always the best. This implies that, as E. F. Schumacher says in his book by the same title, "small is beautiful." Community is, for me here in the woods, a much smaller paradigm than for those who live in towns or in cities like Asheville. And small, as far as I can see—through the windows of my cabin to the pine grove on the far side of Zoro's field—is the only way that works.

(Written in 1981, near the Green River in Polk County, NC)

Native Tongue

Love of place and love of language go hand in hand. Or, as my mentor and friend Zoro has said, "Who you are is all about where you are from." As a boy in Graham County, my first language was what has been called Southern Mountain Speech—a complex blend of Scots, traces of Chaucerian and Elizabethan English, elements of the speech of seventeenth-century immigrants from the British Isles, a witty Irish lyricism, and numerous other forebears. This Appalachian dialect was rich with poetic idioms and colloquialisms, lyrical inflections and rhythms, making it unique as well as almost incomprehensible to any outsider.

I can still remember a rainy Saturday in the Snowbird Supply General Store in Robbinsville and an old fella calling the summer thunderstorm that had me and my buddies holed up inside drinking RC Colas and eating Moon Pies a "sizzly sod-soaker." And later during those years, I heard references to such "thundery weather" as a "Devil's footwasher" and a "nubbin' stretcher." There was no lack of colorful speech. Surrounded by such language, it's no wonder that as early as the third grade I became interested in poetry, and by the fourth grade was attempting to write my own.

But during the summer of 1962, my parents moved our family out of Milltown in Robbinsville to the northern end of the Blue Ridge Parkway just west of Charlottesville, Virginia—thus separating me from the culture and the language I had grown up with. Moving away from the place where I had consciously begun to identify and know myself was my own trail of tears. As I said my good-byes to my Cherokee and Scots-Irish friends and to my life along Snowbird Creek in Graham County and the particular, if not peculiar, culture there, little did I know that I was also saying good-bye to the way I linguistically viewed the world.

As my father uprooted our family time and time again in a march of migration farther and farther north, I lost more and more of my contact and association with my cultural roots. By the time I finished high school in the steel town of Bethlehem, Pennsylvania, I had become little more than the proverbial rolling stone—one that had not had time enough in any one place to gather moss. As years went by and I moved myself farther and farther west on my own, I learned to distance myself from any semblance of a Southern accent—so strong were the prejudices I encountered in other parts of the country against Southern speech. Tired of being castigated and denigrated, I taught myself a generic American speech that was without dialect and therefore without character—a final act of acculturation.

Even though I continued to write poetry, it had become a poetry whose language was unaffected by place. Instead of the organic, lyrical, and idiomatic poetry that might have come easily had I remained in Graham County, I was, by the time I was twenty-five, writing in rhetorical rhythms—a kind of message-based poetry more influenced by Russia and France than by the Appalachian South. People who met me were astonished that I had come from the South, so well had I hidden my past in my newly formed speech.

Only once can I recall slipping and falling back into grace—when I was living an apprentice's life in San Francisco surrounded by many of my Beat Generation idols—on the occasion of meeting in a North Beach café a young musician named Wayde Blair from Berea, Kentucky. Because of his strong Southern drawl, I reverted to old speech patterns that had become buried in my subconscious but broke ground upon hearing his voice and the familiar language. I would, I was told (for I was unaware of the shift), lapse into dialect and even old Appalachian metaphoric idioms when I ran into Wayde and we talked casually about home and the past. Aside from these few San Francisco slips, I remained dialect free.

Now that I am back in western North Carolina, many years after leaving the region as a young teenager, I find that the cultural life, as well as the language, is dying out, as more and more of my generation have moved to larger towns in the region or farther to search for prosperity. One can hear good old Southern Mountain Speech only from the elderly, who decrease in number each year. This being the case, upon returning to the western North Carolina mountains, I found myself gravitating toward elders: Zoro and Bessie Guice, Mose Bradley, Gelolo McHugh.

But now, in my seventies, my recall of my native tongue is faulty, almost nonexistent. I taught myself too well, over the years while I was gone, how to speak sans dialect. And no matter how hard I try to converse on an equal basis with my septuagenarian and octogenarian friends, I am able to give only lip service to my former language.

Yet I have been moved to try to return to my cultural and linguistic roots and to incorporate these back into my daily speech as well as into my writing. I have continued my habit of spending time with the elder generation, as well as the remaining few of my own age who have held tight to traditions, culture, and speech harkening back to the past. In addition to conversations I've had with my neighbors, there have been many memorable exchanges with characters such as the now-deceased Cherokee medicine man Amoneeta Sequoyah and the historian and arts dealer Tom Underwood over on the Qualla Boundary.

I remember a conversation that took place on the back porch of an old mountain sawmill shack looking out into the woods, not long after I had arrived in Polk County fresh from the West Coast. The talk was about gardening, mountain farming, and the old days—of garden sass and wild greens, bird's toe, fiddleheads, speckled dick and lamb's-quarter, mouse's ear, blue root, hen pepper, and woolly breeches. Of cans and pokes. Of sour sop, chitlins, churn rags, and clabber. Of pawpaws, may apples, wild fish, and ramps. Of coal oil and coal-of-fire. Of broom corn and blackstrap. Of bedbugs and rapscallions, rounders, swap slobbers, and swangs.

I've had many colorful conversations over the years with younger-generation yarn spinners such as Paul Rhodes, whose lickety-cut mind and quick wit, coupled with his mountain drawl, have caused me to rar back in my boots with laughter.

Since the beginning, years ago, of my sojourn in the Green River cabin, I've worked to reestablish my identity—my sense of belonging to a particular place and culture—by utilizing Southern Mountain Speech as much as I can, mainly through my writing. While it may be true, metaphorically and metaphysically, that you can't go home again, the fact is that I have come home again and am finding that I can call up the past in bits and pieces and bring it into the present-day voice in which I write. I can pull up Chaucer-era canticles—the triple negatives, the likes of "don't make no never-mind" and "not nary a any"—to grace the images of my poems and fictions.

During the winter months, when I have concentrated time and energy to read and write at length, in poems with titles such as "A Beatnik Wanders into Appalachia and Learns the Language of Earth and Sky," "Crack-Light," and "Who-Shot-John," I've been able to relive the past as well as bring it to light (life) and into the present for myself. When I write "Dig the Big-Eyed Bird in swag or hollow / of locust and locked wood" (which, when translated, means: "You can see God in nature"), I am back in Graham County on the mountain behind my family's house in the Milltown community along Snowbird Creek. And, at the same time, I am here in Tuckasegee experiencing a kind of time travel generated by language—a leap of more than fifty years.

Or when I write "couldn't hold a candle to this wick of words" or "where in tarnation," I can feel strength and satisfaction coming from the heart. In these moments, it seems as if I've got the best of both worlds: past and present. As a gardener of both legumes and language, I know that a time will come when I'll have to lay down my hoe, and my pen, forever. But until that day comes, I aim to keep on diggin'—harvesting the bounty afforded me by good organic food and this beautiful Southern Mountain Speech.

The New Naturalists

(A Southern Appalachian Renaissance)

Such an ocean of wooded, waving, swelling mountain beauty and grandeur is not to be described. Countless forest-clad hills, side by side in rows and groups—all united by curves and slopes of inimitable softness and beauty. Oh, these forest gardens of our Father! What perfection, what divinity, in their architecture!"
—John Muir (*A Thousand Mile Walk to the Gulf*)
on his first impressions of the mountains of western North Carolina

As I gaze from my farmhouse porch at the foot of Shelton Mountain out into the Tuckasegee Valley as witness to much of the natural beauty that has been here, intact, for thousands of years, and ponder Muir's luscious quote about our western North Carolina mountains, I also find myself, at the same time, contemplating more unpleasant thoughts arising from issues that are almost constantly in the local news these days. I'm thinking about the continued desecration of the environment in the form of subdivision development, toxic waste and air pollution, to name only a few of the imposing environmental issues in our region. And I'm wondering: who is going to lead us out of this self-destructive paradigm that was set into motion with the Industrial Revolution and has continued to gather momentum in the last century and a half with the indulgent escalation of free-trade capitalism? I keep asking myself: Where are the "dirt-doctors," the "earth-healers"? Where are the great charismatic voices in government that might begin the work of turning things around? And if not in government, then in society in general—where are our leaders? It seems that there is no one addressing the truly fundamental questions of our day: overpopulation, unchecked and unregulated economic growth, globalism, and land preservation.

If we look back, it has always been the naturalists who have led the way toward more progressive thinking about questions relating to balance and sustainability. It is the nature writers who have positioned themselves on the front lines of the myriad battles to save and preserve the environment. And through their writing, they have sown seeds that sprout as ecological movements, private foundations and governmental programs focused on the long view concerning the welfare of the country's and the planet's landscape and environment. Past generations have looked to the work of Emerson (*Nature*), Thoreau (*Walden*), John Burroughs (*Field and Study*), John Muir (*Steep Trails*), William Bartram (*Travels*), Horace Kephart (*Our Southern Highlanders*), Aldo Leopold (*A Sand County Almanac*), Rachel Carson (*Silent Spring*), Loren Eiseley (*The Night Country*) More recent generations have looked to writers like Robinson Jeffers (*Give Your Heart to the Hawks*), Gary Snyder (*The Practice of the Wild*), and finally in the South, to writers like Birmingham, Alabama native E.O. Wilson

(*In Search of Nature* and *The Creation: An Appeal to Save Life on Earth*), Wendell Berry of the Kentucky backcountry and farming communities (*The Unsettling of America* and *The Gift of Good Land*), and Thomas Berry (*The Dream of the Earth* and *The Great Work*), a North Carolina native who has captured the imagination of the whole environmental movement with his elevated message of spiritual ecology.

Following in the footsteps of Bartram, Kephart, Wilson and the Berrys is a new generation and a new breed of gifted Southern nature writers. "If you would learn the secrets of nature," Thoreau wrote, "you must practice more humanity than others." That credo, more or less, sums up the ethos of these "New Naturalists." They are not only talking the talk, they are walking the walk. They are not only writing an engaged prose and poetry that evokes the spirit of the "Old Naturalists" and their tenets for a sustainable future, but they are quite literally engaged in a kind of activism that is, at once, journalistic, literary, and biographical. They are, through their work and deeds, inspiring, organizing and participating in non-violent actions that provide alternatives to community apathy and destruction of natural habitat.

While writers such as Bill McKibben, Elizabeth Kolbert, Paul Hawken, Amory Lovins, Stewart Brand and Michael Pollan are writing on the subjects of nature and the environment from their homes in the northeast, midwest, southwest or west coast, the South has also "risen up" to be counted as a regional voice espousing preservation and sustainability. In and around the area of the Great Smoky Mountains National Park and the hill country to the north, east, south and west is an exceptionally dedicated, if not devout, group of 60s-generation nature writers worthy of national attention. In a region where the issues of air pollution, water quality, extinction of flora and fauna species, and loss of traditional cultures are front and center, these remarkable writers are not only making a mark on the genre of environmental non-fiction, but they are making a difference.

This group of "Southern Nature Writers," who live in, adjacent to, or have connections with the Katuah Bio-region of North Carolina, is anchored by informal annual reunions under the guise of a "Southern Nature Writers Gathering." Mentored by such voices as Franklin Burroughs (*Billy Watson's Croker Sack*) and the late Jim Kilgo (*Deep Enough for Ivory Bills; The Blue Wall*) is a younger cadre of eco-activist writers and poets who have joined ranks with their elder kinsmen. Writers such as Christopher Camuto (*Another Country; Hunting from Home*) Bill Belleville (*River of Lakes; Losing It All To Sprawl*), Janisse Ray (*Ecology of a Cracker Childhood; Pinhook: Finding Wholeness in a Fragmented Land*), Roger Pinckney (*The Right Side of the River; Blue Roots*), Charles Seabrook ("River in Peril"), Jan DeBlieu (*Hatteras Journal; Meant To Be Wild*) and Dorinda Dallmeyer (*Elemental South*), who is Director of the Environmental Ethics Certificate Program at the University of Georgia. Added to this hub from the "Southern Nature Writers" (go to www.southernnature. org) group and specific to these western North Carolina mountains are our own resident writers. In Jackson County is Burt Kornegay—a map-maker and writer for a variety of state and national "field and stream" publications. He is past President of the North Carolina Bartram Trail Society and has been featured in such nationally respected magazines as *National Geographic, Wildlife*, and *American Hiker* as a wilderness guide who owns Slickrock Expeditions.

In Barnardsville, Buncombe County, just north of Asheville and bordering the Mount Mitchell State Park in the Pisgah National Forest, Will Harlan and his wife live off the grid in a solar-design home surrounded by a growing system of gardens, vineyards and orchards planned and maintained with the principles of Permaculture in mind. Will was Editor and writer for *Blue Ridge Outdoors* (based in Charlottesville, Virginia), a staunch supporter of the grassroots organization The Canary Coalition (whose focus is on air-quality issues in the region), and is a world-class Xtreme-terrain marathon runner.

In Swain County, there is poet-turned-naturalist and journalist George Ellison, whose knowledge of nature lore and Native American history in this region is approaching the level of being encyclopedic. His books *Mountain Passages* and *A Blue Ridge Nature Journal*, newspaper columns, frequent nature-walk workshops, and contributions to the living folklore of the region have been and continue to be invaluable in educating the public about its past as well as its invasive present. His stamp appears on two of the seminal tomes of Southern Appalachian natural and cultural history: *Mooney's History, Myths, and Sacred Formulas of the Cherokees*, and *Kephart's Our Southern Highlanders*, for which he has been honored by being asked to write new, updated Introductions.

Just next door in Jackson County along the Tuckasegee River, whitewater enthusiast, wilderness and recreation writer and poet John Lane owns land in a remote cove off John's Creek Road in the Caney Fork community of Cullowhee. There he has built a beautiful reconstructed one-room saw-mill shack, which he uses as a writer's retreat and where he spends his spare time and his summers in close proximity to the headwaters of the Nantahala and Chattooga rivers. Lane is actively involved in water and land development issues in the region and has authored a book on the Chattooga River (*Chattooga: Descending into the Myth of Deliverance River*). His journal-entry book *Weed Time*, which was written in the environs of Whittier while living up Camp Creek Road, is a snap-shot of place-based awareness. His investigative journalism in behalf of the ecological issues here in the mountains and down on the other side of the "Blue Wall" in the South Carolina piedmont, where he calls Spartanburg County home, are written thoughtfully in attack mode, leaving no stone unturned. While his journalistic work is clever, aggressive and geologic, his poetry written about the western North Carolina mountains is equally as gentle, sensitive and lyric.

Up in Watauga County, the movement for a sustained environment has been enjoined by anthropologist/writer/activist Harvard Ayers at Appalachian State in books such as *An Appalachian Tragedy: Air Pollution and Tree Death in The Eastern Forests of North America* (Sierra Club) and *Polluted Parks in Peril: The Five Most Air-Polluted National Parks in the United States*. His work on behalf of clean air coalitions here in western North Carolina has been influential, if not essential in North Carolina's passage, in June of 2001, of the groundbreaking "Clean Smokestacks Act," setting an important precedent for the rest of the country.

And in Macon County, over in the Cowee community there's Brent Martin (*A Shout in the Woods* and *Poems From Snow Hill Road*) and Lamar Marshall. Brent Martin has been the regional representative for The Wilderness Society. He has been a director for other environmental groups in the Southern Appalachians region, including Georgia Forest Watch (based in the mountains of north Georgia) and the Little Tennessee Land Trust of the Great Smoky Mountains. He's almost always out in the woods, searching and mapping old and new terrain for potential preservation, while looking for stands of old growth forest and tracing issues that threaten the wilderness areas of western North Carolina.

Also residing in Macon County in the remote Alarka Watershed, where he grows a large garden, is Lamar Marshall. Lamar originally hails from Alabama and is something of a legend there as a woodsman, trapper and relentless activist for the preservation of wilderness; he is the founder of Wild South and its magazine of the same name. Having moved to the cooler environs of the Smokies, he has taken up the cause of the Cherokee and is working with the Tribe on an extensive, high-profile, grant-funded mapping project to discover, identify, document and protect the Indian trails, old village sites, and nature-related survival systems (such as fishing weirs) misplaced or lost to Cherokee history. His work as trail-blazer, explorer, map-maker and writer here in the western North Carolina mountains has only served to expand his legendary reputation and his "range" as someone working with words to preserve and protect our region.

While the amount of work to be done in cleaning up and preserving our environment here in the mountains of North Carolina and in the surrounding foothills and piedmont areas of adjacent states might, at times, seem overwhelming, these "new naturalists" and others like them seem to be more than equal to the task. This is a focused and dedicated "wild bunch" who have taken on the heavy yoke of unchecked progress, growth and development, and, in exemplary bio-regional fashion, with strong backs are pulling the ecology wagon here in the Southern Appalachians. "May it continue"....as the old Cherokee ceremonial chant says: this nature-activist tradition, this beautiful place, and these people who live here well.

A House in the Valley

Much like the history of the Tuckasegee Baptist Church, which began over in the Caney Fork community before moving to the Tuckasegee Valley one hundred and eighty years ago, I, too, lived on Caney Fork and then moved over the mountain to Tuckasegee. In truth, like many people who live now in this valley and in Little Canada, I'm an "outlander," having grown up in Graham County (Robbinsville). So, as folks here in the mountains would say, "You're not from here, are you?" When it's 38 degrees outside, it's 38 degrees inside this 150-year-old mountain house that sits down in the Tuckasegee River flood plain literally a stone's throw from the river, here in the Tuckasegee Valley that was settled and occupied by Cherokee and pre-Cherokee peoples and then later by several generations of Hoopers and Moses before other families and occupants moved here.

What was originally a basic two-story, wood-framed house with an outhouse in the back yard is now a house with aluminum siding to which there have been two major add-ons since then, and the bathroom, thank goodness, has been moved indoors. My first impression of the old home place when I moved in here thirty-three years ago in 1993 was that it was pretty run down and was going to need a lot of work and tender loving care. Much of Highway 281, which runs in front of our house, was still unpaved, much as it had been when the house was built. So, as soon as I moved in, I began making suggestions regarding the kind of changes that would be amenable to my landlords and at the same time would make the place comfortable, sustainable, and somehow our own. In the intervening years a new metal roof has been put on the house, the entire upstairs and downstairs has been sheetrocked, painted, and trimmed, the well pump has been replaced, and most of the plumbing has been replumbed.

Outdoors, I've landscaped the entire acre around the house with perennial flower gardens and various trees, shrubs, and fruit arbors, as well as various copycat Japanese landscaping ideas that I've stolen from the many Zen garden books that I read during a period when I was fascinated by all that and trying to implement some of it here around this mountain home. I've also enlarged and improved the house garden—that includes building raised beds and installing an irrigation system. The garden plot, although being a lot of work, has fed my partner and me through every summer, fall, winter, and spring since we've been here, and in exceptional years provided me with additional income with the organic produce I've been able to grow and sell to local restaurants and at the Sylva Farmer's Market.

In the winter I heat with wood and have since my first winter here thirty-three years ago. Someone once asked me how much I was paying for logs or a cord of split wood. My immediate response to their question was, "If you have to pay for firewood in these mountains, then you're not paying attention." Since moving to Jackson County in 1984, I've not spent a cent on firewood—so available is it constantly from any number of local sources. An additional source of heat here in this house is from the passive solar heat that comes from what was once a front porch that faced the road along the river and has now become a south-facing greenhouse. In other words, thanks to the kindness of our landlords, we've treated this providential rental property as if it were our own home.

"You could see between the floorboards on the second floor to the first floor below," eighty-five-year-old Ethel Bradley Moses, who had grown up in this house when she was just eleven years old, told me when she and her sister Nettie Bradley and Ethel's daughter Cherrie Moses visited here a few years ago. "And in the big flood of 1940, this house almost got washed away," Ethel added. And I remembered a story that Mary Jo Hooper Cobb had told me when recalling the flood. "My little sister," she said, "was so upset at all the damage the flood had done that she just blurted out, 'Jesus is as bad as the Boogerman!'" Ethel then told us a story of how in 1911 the entire Tuckasegee River froze over and how the horses and wagons crossed the river on the ice. And then there was the story of their old laying hen named "Old Crip" that would come through the front door into the house every morning and lay an egg inside the kitchen cupboard down near the floor.

The original stone chimney on this house from the nineteenth century is still standing (even though no longer functional) like an ancient obelisk where chimney sweeps and occasional boomers nest in between the old river stones of the chimney and keep us awake at night—a reminder of the era and the age of this building as one of the first home places, along with the Hooper house on the south side of the valley and Mary Jo Hooper's house over on the west slope, to be built in this valley in the early to mid-1800s. Since that time there have been many owners and renters, including Rigdons, McCoys (who the old swimming hole, "the McCoy Hole," in the river is still named after), Barnes, Wiggins, and then a Col. Hill who owned the house and land before selling it to the current owners, the Wilcoxes.

It's 45 degrees outside today, and it's 48 degrees upstairs here in my attic room study as I try to write this, clad in long johns, wool shirt, and heavy sweater. There are no cracks in the floor now like there were eighty years ago, and the floor is covered in strange floral-patterned linoleum squares. The walls are clothed in that thin faux paneling that is supposed to look like real wood. From here I sit and look out the two windows on the eastern wall and watch what goes on in the yard, the garden, the fields, and in the sky. From these two portals (that serve as my "eyes" on the outdoor world) I have watched a family of bobcats bathe in the birdbaths, observed bald eagles and a full-grown black bear in the large walnut tree in the yard, seen foxes and deer and a thousand birds that use these grounds as a regular daily passage, played peekaboo with the hummingbirds that arrive on the same day as the morel mushrooms appear every year in the spring. It's a great view—with Shelton Mountain in the background—and there's always a lot of action and sometimes a great show. "Your place feels so comfortable and relaxing," we often hear our friends say, especially in winter when the wood stove with its large glass door is cranked up and putting off an inviting and luxuriant heat.

Over the years, I have tried to figure out just what it is that gives this place such an aura of calmness and tranquility. At first I thought it was my passion for Zen gardens that was giving the place its charm, or maybe the ambiance of our living on a sixty-acre mountain farm with bright red barns and outbuildings and a small herd of sheep and goats grazing in the surrounding fields. In the end, I think I have found the answer in books I have read on the science of geomancy and feng shui. The classic definition of feng shui is "the art of living in harmony with the land, and deriving the greatest benefit, peace and prosperity from being in the right place at the right time." The feng shui manuals on "sacred landscape" all confirm that our little mountain home along the Tuckasegee River is situated in and fits the profile for an ideal landscape for "good feng shui" or positive energy. We are "located at the foot of a dragon-shaped mountain (Shelton Mountain), protected from high winds by a northern screen of hills or trees, a place in which streams and rivers meander slowly, and which nestles in the embrace of hills rather like an armchair, with a view preferably to the south." Not only are we and our visiting friends always enamored of the calming influence of the house itself, but the wildlife here is abundant and seems to be at peace and in accord with us and our little watershed in general—a watershed which includes not only the Tuckasegee River but an underground wellspring only a few yards from the house and a runoff stream that comes off Shelton Mountain when it rains.

All things considered, it would certainly seem that I have come to and am living in "the right place at the right time." While there are multiple feeders that I keep stocked in sunflower seeds and various grains for a huge range of bird species (including an occasional misguided guinea hen or two that have wandered away from Mary Jo Hooper's farm down the road and across the river), I also hand-feed the foxes cracked corn and feed the raptors, bobcats, and cougars (yes, cougars) with occasional squirrels, rabbits, rodents, and other "garden scavengers" and/or house pests, as necessary. Otherwise, the wild creatures here seem content to fend for themselves and to hang out in a place where the earth energies are inviting and they feel safe. Or as *The Living Earth Manual of Feng-Shui* puts it, "The site is referred to as a 'lair' because the position of the house site is as essential to man's wellbeing as the selection of a lair is to an animal." As "outlanders" or "furriners," my partner and I have embraced both the cultural history and the environmental ecosystem here in the Tuckasegee Valley and have come to know and be accepted by our neighbors (still mostly Hoopers and Moses) whose genealogy goes back for generations. There is a true sense of community here, and we all strive to be "neighborly" and to live harmoniously and as sustainably as possible in a place that is not only beautiful but has given life to humans, plants, and animals for centuries, if not millennia. And we all try to live here with respect and in gratitude. May it continue. Or, as the pastor of Tuckasegee Baptist, Jack Hinson, says, "It's great to be in Tuck-a-see-gee!"

The Wild Work

It's good to work—I love work, work and play are one. All of us will come back again to hoe in the ground, or gather wild potato bulbs, or hand-adze a beam, or skin a pole, or scrape a hive—we're never going to get away from that. We'll always do that work. That work is always going to be there.

—Gary Snyder
from: *The Real Work*

When Gary Snyder signs his letters to me, "yours in the wild work," I know what he means. He's talking about organizing a local watershed institute, preparing presentations for the board of county commissioners, participating in forest-fire training sessions with the volunteer fire department, writing another poem for his *Mountains and Rivers Without End* cycle, planting a garden, making a firebreak, splitting firewood, sewing beads onto a peyote-meeting fan, putting a water pump on his old flatbed truck. The highbrow and the lowbrow of the work of self-sufficiency. The intellect intensely engaged alongside the forearm.

I watched him and his neighbors attentively during my years living up on the San Juan Ridge in northern California—the way they worked as solitaries and the way they worked as a community. It was no easy thing scratching a life out of the rough climate and terrain of the Sierra foothills along the Yuba River. And the word "work" took on a new meaning for me as I wiped the sweat from my brow working and playing alongside Gary's friends and my new neighbors.

But there's work and then there's "the wild work." While it's a fine line that separates the two (if, indeed, they should be separated at all), the wild work, for me, is more about time spent in thought and deed in the wild world. In the world of nature. In the wilderness. This emphasis on wildness and wilderness comes from my own upbringing and my memories of those years.

Those memories are juxtaposed with days like today, when the wind is blowing from the west and I can hear the incessant roar of the mufflerless trucks on Highway 281 all day long—which, with the windows open, sounds like it's right outside my door. This particular unpleasant disruption puts me on the defensive, and I yearn for an even simpler, quieter life—even farther from the fray and noise of the world and even deeper into the undeveloped and uninhabited woods that, ironically, are owned by Duke Power Company and border the Tuckasegee River.

My initiation into the world of wildness came during my childhood years growing up on Snowbird Creek in Graham County, North Carolina. Snowbird Creek, the woods, the abundant wildlife, and the free-form, free-ranging relationship the young Cherokee boys and I had with this natural world were

all there in my backyard—just outside the door of the little house where I was reared, irrespective of my parents' livelihood and values, as a child of nature.

My own essential and permanent social and environmental values were formed during those years, as were friendships, some of which have also lasted a lifetime. And it was there, I believe, that wildness became a part of my own personal bloodline—part of my genetic coding. Those were the barefoot years, running unimpeded and uninhibited through a seemingly boundless, wooded, watery, loamy, mossy, fern-resplendent, and blooming photosynthetic Eden. Surrounded in every direction by clean air, drinkable water, and the green silence and great solitude of the woods, my friends and I used the creeks and forests as a playground, where we were as free and at ease as were the animals.

While a good many families in our little mountain community eked out their livings working in the lumber industry—the main employer in the county—I was living a charmed life, oblivious to the unpleasant issues associated with the logging business and such specters as clear-cutting, which is on the tip of every tongue here in western North Carolina these days. The wilderness that surrounded my home across the road from Snowbird Creek was the source of my sense of freedom. In the shadows of the deciduous rain forest, I became conscious for the first time of the paradox of being anonymous there amongst the trees and, at the same time, of being so very visible, vulnerable, and known as a part of the community of wild animals and species that lived there so freely. At that point I began living, consciously, a dual life: the life I lived when I was with my family, when I was in school, when I was at church—in short, the life I lived in and around the human community—and the life I lived on my own when I was alone in the woods.

When I think back on those years, I think it has to be that pristine boyhood experience that has led me to these woods and this experience along the Tuckasegee River here in Jackson County. Why else would I be here? Why else would I have left northern California and the camaraderie of kindred kind? The answer to these questions could be nothing other than an arcane yet symbiotic calling that has come psychogenetically from my memories of wild youth spent not all that far from here. What other explanation could there be for my bizarre behavior? For leaving behind a congenial nature-based community for this quasi-hermit's life in the woods of conservative Southern Baptist North Carolina?

When Gary Snyder told me to "go home," at first I felt insulted, spurned. I took it to mean that he thought I was out of place there in the San Juan community. That I wasn't welcome. Didn't fit in. An outsider—something I had felt most of my life after being uprooted from my Graham County home as a boy. So, I rebelled by burying his remark in my subconscious and ignoring it, or at least trying my best to, which was no easy thing, as it had come from someone I looked up to as a mentor and teacher. Yet here I am, back in the

North Carolina mountains. Home. Where now I am sitting, thinking back in the other direction, over a time-bridge that has lengthened from months to years, to when I lived on the site of an old Maidu ceremonial village, rich with old oaks (from which the natives had gathered acorns to make ooti—a kind of porridge that was their main dish), artifacts, and spirits-of-place who, more often than not, made themselves known in all manner of unpredictable if not unsettling ways. Back then I lived alongside a very different community of wildlife from what is familiar to me here—coyote, cougar, condor, eagle, weasel, and what seemed an overabundance of rattlesnake and deer.

I lived in that place in a Plains Indian tipi under a five-hundred-year-old cedar tree amidst a community of humans that included farmers, home builders, moccasin makers, musicians, river rafters, magazine editors, and Zen meditators. In that community I was allowed to live a kind of Anglo-Indian fantasy, where I rode a wild stallion bareback over and through the northern California hill country, coming home from those riding excursions to tend fields of comfrey, popcorn, and garlic and to make cheese and yogurt from the milk of goats. As I sit here looking back on it, I can see that not only was that period something of a return to my past and the pristine connections I had made with the natural world here in western North Carolina as a boy, but it served as a means of making even deeper impressions on my inner psychic and psychological wildernesses. Having developed a more mature and objective eye by the time I arrived in the Sierra foothills, I was able, in that wild yet nurturing environment wedding human with nature, more clearly to search for and see the big picture where the natural universe was concerned, and how it played off the microcosmic world with relative ease and balance.

I sit here in my rocker, with the wood stove lit and the front door of this mountain house wide open, in a warm womb, and think fondly of those Maidu village days and of the reinhabitory community into which I was accepted. And out of which I was thrown, gently and lovingly, in order that I might find my way back to my true home here in the western North Carolina woods.

The years of experience and awareness garnered in the backcountry of the Sierras and earlier during my Graham County boyhood, I have brought back with me into this one hundred and fifty-year-old house. For almost thirty-five years this has been my home, where I am again amongst the familiar faunal faces of my youth: black bear, wild turkey, hedgehog, peregrine falcon, gray fox, ruffed grouse, blacksnake, copperhead, and the ever-present crows. With the gift of a roof over my head, enough cleared land to garden, and few interruptions or temptations from the outside world, I have set up house and garden to take Thoreau's Walden experience even more self-sufficiently into the Smoky Mountains countryside. To try to discover firsthand the organic and natural rhythms of the God-given world, as well as the ritual essences of self-sufficiency, self-confidence, and the purging of psychological fear. Where on full-moon nights I sit by the fire in deep thought, contemplating a physics of wildness based on commonsense familiarity and observation borne of a life lived at the (true) speed of life. A speed borne of wilderness. A life lived doing the wild work.

The wild work, like "the real work" Snyder talks about, is borne of necessity and caring. Caring for what lives around us and what sustains us. Caring implies protecting. For if we should not protect that which sustains us, then what are we left with but our own wits and clumsy devices that feign to approximate what the natural world does as a matter of course? The real and wild work is what we humans do with our intellect and efforts to organize and improvise ways of maintaining some modicum of balance with the natural world, allowing us a life of relative peace and possibility and, in good times, even a sense of security. Without this inner peace that comes with a deep inner knowing that we are at one with the wild world around us, there can really be no sense of security, and therefore we are not at rest but rather are restless, fearful, tired. And we know from history what havoc is wreaked from fear and fatigue. So, while fear and fatigue are inherently present in those few of us who attempt to live self-sufficiently on the land, we do try to minimize those weakened and deluded states of body and mind by giving ourselves a fair chance at a noble life of living at peace amidst the ordered anarchy of the wild.

Snyder himself defines the real work as being: "What we really do. And what our lives are. And if we can live the work we have to do, knowing that we are real, and that the world is real, then it becomes right. And that's the 'real' work: to make the world as real as it is, and to find ourselves as real as we are within it. It is what is to be done. To take the struggle on without the least hope of doing any good. To check the destruction of the interesting and necessary diversity of life on the planet so that the dance can go on a little better for a little longer."

Taking life one day at a time is what I think he's getting at here. For my part, I have taken and given, on this day, all that I have. I've fed the wild birds, created a five-day stew that I have simmering on the wood stove, chopped up a week's worth of kindling and night wood, sewed buttons back on my winter vest, walked to the nearby post office here in the Tuckasegee Valley, and written it all down in the detailed journal I am keeping of the seasonal transition from winter to spring. It has all been done wildly, yet with love.

It's past dark and time for bed. I stick one last round of ironwood into the small box wood stove, shut down the air vent and the damper for the night. My last act of wild work for the day.

A Saint Among Us

I was one of the lucky ones. I met and befriended Thomas Berry on Earth Day in the late 1980s during his youthful middle age and at the beginnings of his meteoric rise to prominence as an author of books on spiritual ecology—books that raised the bar on the beginnings and what would become the awareness and movement regarding what was then being labeled "global warming" and what is now a full-blown climate change movement that is global in scope and scale. During those years following the publication of his lynchpin book of nonfiction titled *The Dream of the Earth*, and while I was making my living as a freelance writer, I met with him and did a series of interviews for various regional and national publications. As years went by, I ended up reviewing almost all of his books that were to follow, which included *The Great Work* and *The Universe Story*. In the end, Thomas Berry and I became friends up until the time of his death in 2009. He graciously wrote endorsements for a couple of my own books during those years, which—now looking back at age seventy-six—I consider the highlights of my career.

Thomas Berry, who was born and raised in Greensboro, North Carolina, had a life unlike anyone I've ever met or known. In *Thomas Berry: A Biography*, three of his friends who knew him well have combined their knowledge and talents to create a comprehensive story of this man's remarkable life and legacy. We start with his early life and follow him through his student years and to his induction into the Passionist Order of the Catholic Church. From there we follow him as an ordained priest and monk to outposts around the world (China and Europe) before eventually returning to the United States to teach at Fordham University, Barnard College, and Columbia University, and then to his focus on human and Earth history and the founding of the Riverdale Center for Religious Research along the Hudson River in New York State and consequently the writing of his books on helping to restore the continuity of humans with the natural world—replacing the modern alienation from nature with a sense of intimacy, responsibility, and reverence.

So, in the end, how do we access this man's life and legacy? I have used the term "saint" to describe him here, to characterize what he has left for humanity to ponder and process as we go forward into the dark of these stormy and troubling times. If you look at the facts, the overall arc, and the accomplishments of Thomas Berry's life, one can easily compare him to other great spiritual beings and leaders in human history. Saint Francis of Assisi comes to mind, first and foremost, followed by other spiritual masters such as the Persian Sufi masters Hafiz, Rumi, and Kabir, or teachers like Teilhard de Chardin, whom Berry much admired. No matter how you qualify his achievements or to whom you compare him, he stands alone as the old soul that he was and as someone who lived a life that one can only call admirable, if not exemplary. Or can I use

the term "saintly" again? His personality and concerns, if not his writings, are certainly of that caliber, in my humble opinion. The authors of his biography describe him like this: "As someone who had a deep feeling for human suffering and a profound concern for the destruction of the life systems of the planet, he was unfailingly kind, unstintingly generous. He had an irrepressible joy that spilled over into hospitality to whomever he met. People felt they were his close friends even after one meeting. He had an unusual charisma as well as a prophetic voice that could thunder at those disrupting Earth's ecosystems and roar at those institutions failing to respond. His criticisms of education, politics, business, and religion were usually scathing. But he was always identifying those who were change-makers on the borders of the establishments. He could not abide the withering of the Earth's beauty, the diminishment of its biodiversity, the marginalization of its struggling peoples. He brooded over the tragedies humans were inflicting or enduring."

At a time when the world is in dire need of charismatic spiritual and sociopolitical leaders, when we look around there aren't many, if any, in sight. But perhaps such a person can be identified and can rise to such a position posthumously. That being the case, one can only hope that the values and ideas espoused by Thomas Berry will find a place of prominence and a very large readership at a time when the elevation in human consciousness and spiritual awareness is paramount. Finally, Thomas left us with a simple yet profound mantra as to how to live our lives: "Live—fully. Laugh—often. Forgive—instantly. Love—always." So, if you are someone who likes to read biographies, or even if you aren't, I urge you to pick up one of his books and read it cover to cover. If you don't come away with a greater awareness and compassion for humankind and planet Earth, I'll be a monkey's uncle.

Part II

The Aristocracy of the Wild

> *All good things are wild and free.*
> —Henry David Thoreau

It's not the money,
it's the wilderness that turns me on.
It's not the fame,
it's the songs I have learned from birds.
It's not the sex,
it's the orgasm of a windy day.
The taste of wild grapes.
The smell of honeysuckle.
The sound of thunder in the hills.
This is my inheritance.
The things that have made me rich.
The blue blood in my veins.

It's not the prestige or the privilege,
it's her lips that turn me on.
It's not the mansions,
it's the time I have spent in caves.
It's not the power,
it's the cougar's call of caution.
The bleating of lambs.
The Lilacs.
The Asters,.
The Lyreleaf Sage.
This is my aristokratia.
The things that gave me heart.
The nobility of my pale skin.

It's not the class or the style,
it's the silk of her skin that turns me on.
It's not the authority,
it's the river after torrential rain.
It's not the elegance,
it's the genius of diversity.
The community of ants.
The comb of the bees.
The nest of hummingbirds.
These.

Walking the Woods

S ay the word "walk" and she's out the door
H eaded for the woods and any path that
E nters a green landscape that
G oes on forever and never ends
O r wants to hold houses on its flanks or
E ven its meadows where she is lost in the delicate
S unshine warming the leaves of fan-veined plants as she
E nters the under story of Buckeye, Hickories and Thornless Plums.
V iburnums blaze the trail near Flame Azalea and Fire Pink as
E arly spring morphs into early summer and
R edbuds with resin and ring scar come to life like
Y oung flower girls at nature's nuptials
W ith lanceolate leaders and lobed leaves as palmates
H aving only fun on an outing into the
E verything of where the node of nightmares ends and the
R eal takes shape in the midvein of Nightshade wanting to be Ragwort in
E very step she takes past Pipevine and Bluecurls, by Bloodroot and
B ouncing Bet where bees hover before making their way to Foam Flower and
U p the trail past waterfalls to where Black Birch house Nuthatch, Grosbeak and Winter Wren.
T here on Angel Moss she sits to savor silence and the
L one whistle of wind that takes her to places
O nly she can go and goes willing to be wild
V ery close to wilderness and all that is perfect and protected
E ven as she eats wild blueberries and watercress she has found in canopied
S unlight along the way.
T hen as crows call, she rises and makes haste to the top of the
H ill where topsoil turns to Galax and Loosestrife and in
E very direction there is her favorite view of ridge lines
W andering east in lingering breast lines not unlike her
O wn under thin cloth that has given milk to children
O ld enough to have their own who will grow up into the out-of-
D oors and be taken to the woods and
S hown what it is to move forward along paths and be wild.

The Idiot's Wind

a long haiku, for Steve Earle

Idiot wind... blowing down the back roads headin' south...
It's a wonder that you still know how to breathe.
—Bob Dylan, "Idiot Wind," *Blood on the Tracks*

Is this the best we can do?
Turn wonderful air
into a hurricane of haze—
Turn landscape and vistas
into pictures painted for the blind—
Fill pink lungs of children
with black space—
Make soot we breathe
surreal salt in the food of film noir,
for profit and at any price.

Is this the best we can do?
From a pile of coal
make heat—
Make light
from a hill of peat—
From hell-bent   to heartache
hookers of energy   in bed with the rich;
the blood of the poet in a Blue Ridge ditch,
for profit and at any price.

Is this the best we can do?
Stay cool in the face of fire—
The gift of mankind:
an eternal pyre—
Using the mind
as a political gyre,
for profit and at any price.
Hands and head in a vice.
Denying Nature not two times, but thrice.
Fanning the flames of dry ice.
Use poison in food and calling it spice.
For what profit? What price?

Is this the best we can do?
Only an idiot
would try to make love to the wind.
Would inhale oxygen and call it CO2.
Or think sun and moon
would come from some Yahweh living in another place.
Would kiss the lips of bombs and call them sweet.
Or move their home to somewhere in outer space.
This   is grace?
This   the human race?

We can do better than this.

What *Is* Is

after John O'Donohue, in memory

To know what the Is of something is,
you need to know its name.
To have heard the music
in its voice or
seen the color of its pain.

When I watch the sky,
it is what is behind the weather
that I want to see.
What is at the center of circumference
and at the aurora of light. To know
the heart's soul. The heart of stone.
The eye of the storm. The still in the stream.
The bear's growl.
The vowels in the cooing of the dove…

If you want to describe this,
say what is spoken
yet beyond words.
What you want is
when your words and what you are saying
appear as raindrops and
birds on the wing.
From nothing   something is manifest
and appears.
What was missing is suddenly
there.
Something that was distant,
suddenly near.
In this knowing
try to be this and
remember you are here.

What Words Are Worth

after William Wordsworth

What words were worth will be only the forgotten
memory of bells ringing in the bones
that moan of money or the meaning of time
that time has tortured and taken away from its youth
when youth was a time younger than age and
older than what New was to progress or profit,
was better than the buildings or the business
that are the butts of jokes that never laugh or
linger close to the heart fourscore.
BUT THERE'S MORE!
More money or minds smaller than any blue in ink
will ever be for what ain't the truth in a lie and
is the laughing stock of an age of reason,
of over-kill, of everything aimed at the eyes
that don't blink only stare into the space of
a blank wall or electric page that is anything but white or
ever will be any thing for anything less than
a dime anymore when all that's left is the
leftovers of those that are rich and never romantic
like words were to Wordsworth and to me
who sits in a room on the third floor of
anywhere where there is a window and a desk and
forever is as far as the I can see.

Evensong

Even the evening's song sings
acappella after all
the lips of loudness have gone mad
and silence sounds like so much
empty breeze between branches
of old trees
too tired to fight the air or
any ambush of guns gunning down
children, churchmen, or common thieves.
Will a round of ammo give our nightmares
wings? Will things?
Even the aftermath of nouns
won't give verbs their rights to sing,
to hold high C in their hand and say
"I am"
or
"I am not alone in this night."
Night that no longer leads to daylight
out of darkness deader than doornails
that do the job on anyone that wants in
or wants in on the deal of
high priests and mogul kings
cornering the market on the flim-flam
of finance and flicks.
Not even the Minister of Culture
will admit to the adultery of cash
or that singing is a song,
a song sung to fame
that leaves a farmhouse in ruin,
proud men homeless
or runes in a heap of rust
rotting like the lack of language
creepy as cash-registers
in a life of lost poems and machines.

a beatnik wanders into appalachia
and learns the language of the earth and sky

Climbing cold streams' wet weave of root
& rock a warm murmur breathes beneath
a pool of song where water and wilt shine
on green tendrils moist with deep moss
and dew.

Dig the dance of vine
climbing circle of stone.
Dig the blue bloom of rose
cut to caress torrents of rotting soil.
Dig the ripe wave of evening that touches flame
& breaks blood's slow boil of mulch & rain.

Walking green trees' coppered limbs of stairs
& canopy a thrush of whistles rises in
a swoon of sunlight when thunder slaps and
color arcs in clouds' turbid mood of limber logs and leaves.

Dig the skiff of snow that preeks soft
near the rabbit's lair.
Dig the Big-Eyed Bird in swag or hollow
of locust and locked wood.
Dig the heave of new ground and the golden comb
of honey with winter rye.
Dig the dogtick and the rowan tree.
Dig the sky!

Mingus Mill

Over rock and gravel bed
Mingus Creek runs fast through the tall trees.
Diverted by a makeshift dam,
it turns to the right
and into a millrace lined with boards.
An "Appalachian aqueduct" I call it
as I walk along the man-made stream.
Race becomes a flume
and flume becomes water's tressle
downhill to the mill.

Old man Mingus owned the land,
but Sion Early planned and built the building
to custom-grind the grains and corn.
Inside the mill
with its hoppers, boxes and large white stones,
the wheat was threshed in bolting chests
and squirrel-cage smut machines
only to lie a foot deep on the floor.
The corn ground and stored in bins,
sifted and bagged for sale—

With turbine rusted and penstock in ill-repair,
the miller says he can't grind
my Cherokee corn.
"Won't be millin' 'til the spring—
when we've raised enough money
to 'aplace the pipe and put some power in them gears,"
he says in apologetic tone.
This means I'll have to go, now, to Tennessee
to grind my blue and white corn.

Almost dusk, the miller closes
the gate on the flume
and the water flows
over the old wood boards like a falls.

William Bartram Goes Hiking in the Wilderness And Falls in Love With a Beautiful Girl

I am William Bartram
exploring the lines in your skin.
Lines of rivers. Lines of streams.
Varicose of valleys.
Valleys that are home for grazing elk,
my fingers. Feeling for freedom. Feeling for names.
Cataloochee, Chalohuma, Clingman's Dome.
Cliffs that shine in deep sunlight
reflecting your face. Woodlands
turning red October when you blush
as I feed on your ears.
O Love, from where did you come?
A maiden made from these woods.

When I make maps I paint landscapes of
rivers and ravines. Cheoah, Cullasaja, Cataloochee Creek.
Portraits of your body
like it lies next to me in the wild of fallen leaves.
A wilderness wet with a flood of tears
from morning dew. Something done
for the sake of doing   and done right
to be left for future lovers unloved in the night.

O Love, you have come to me untamed.
A leopard lept here from extinct stars.
A gallery of galaxies grazing in this valley's grass.
Like fields of wild strawberries being gathered by virgin girls.
A lover's nightmare. Yet you are a woodsman's dream.
Eyes mascaraed with lobelia and chanterelles.
Skin tasting of saffron, caramel and forest loam.

Here, in this cartography of kisses
there are no straight lines that lead to you.
Curved space the shortest route to your eyes.
Curved time the entrance to our dreams.

The Names

for Charles Frazier

Whether it was the thirteen moons that night
in the cold, mountain sky,
or the woods lit up with gollywhoppers of light,
it was what we remembered as Halloween for
the rest of our lives as something so spooky
that to even say the word "haint" was a spell
we cast on ourselves and all our friends.
Even with all that on our minds,
we ran with our pokes to every house on the street
hoping for a handout, the miracle of money,
or candy to go with our bottled dope.
We were just yardbabies, then, but
now, when we write in the night
we kindle the thought of flames—the names—
that kept us warm as a whang of likker or
woozy as when we read a wishbook
or what we writ in blank books under cover of
what were our wildest dreams.
Stickerweed.
Step rock.
Stay-place.
Squinch owl.
Stingy vine.
Sheepshower.
Shoemake.
Sweet fern.
Sour mash.
Stump-water.
Snowbird.
Snakeroot.
Shuck-beans.
Shoo-fly.
Sow belly.
Sassafrack.
Shame-briar.
She-balsam.
Sugar tree
and sweet-talk
by country boys at play-parties
and all our caigy games.

No More Nationalism

N either the Nothing or the Everything has time
O r patience for the indulgence of power that is

M ore than what each human enjoys that is
O pen to comfort, peace and light
R ather than "more for me" in the
E ternal race for profit at any price.

N ot even the ant or the elephant needs to
A dd more money or mayhem to its
T ribe, but rather is more concerned with others'
I ncapacity to enjoy in place of oneself.
O nly when we place the ego in the trash and
N ot enthralled with only the "me" or "mine" of our own good can we
A ssimilate the scope and scale of what the sun-
L ight and the horizon can bring. None of this
I n nations or states or armies or money in the bank.
S o go outside and dance to the music of who we really are and were
M eant to be. All waves. All in the same sea.

Fall in Big Cataloochee Valley / An Ecology

for Wayne Caldwell

For a hundred and fifty years only one road out of 'Big Cataloochee,' dug by hand. Built on buffalo trails that crawl like a blacksnake on a rough-cut wall up Half Acre Ridge to Cove Creek Gap. In the valley the small elk herds graze side by side with turkey and crows. Sharing fields that Caldwells cleared on the bottoms 'long Shanty Branch. Along Cataloochee Creek, the old church and schoolhouse stand alone like widowed ghosts with open doors that answer the bugling of the bison-sized males like Sunday's bells. How many Caldwells, Messers and Woodys lived here hidden between these two old hills? And how many elk, deer, bear and beaver once called this place home? Now we drive by in large gas machines looking for graves. Spoiling for a fight and the crash of antlers from the rutting bulls. Going where the history of humans and the flora for ancient animals have forever been. From what the hell these eyes have seen: the subtle passing of the green.

The Change

Where are we going? What will we do? And who will make the change?
Will it be me or will it be you? How far will we extend the range?

Start with the chorus. Add the refrain. Let's stop the bleeding. Let's stop the pain.
Lets elevate smart folks. Lets ignore all the dumb.
Here in this country where we're building walls and we've become comfortably numb.
What we need is a dose of the 60s. When we were all happy and high.
When we knew what we knew and "what ain't the truth is a lie."
So don't be shy and please don't cry. Just stand up to be counted and give it a try.
Don't even ask 'why'. Just say goodbye to all those bold losers that are all about 'my'.
Cause this ain't a time for some pie in the sky.

Where are we going? What will we do? And who will make the change?
Will it be me or will it be you? How far will we extend the range?

Lets ring the bell, sing the spell and dig the well of hope.
There's no time to lose and we gotta choose for whom that we're going to vote.
Let's make headline news, stop singing the blues and sing a purer note.
So come on now I'll show you. To where we need to go.
I'll be the lighthouse beacon. I'll be the arrow's bow.
And no more talk of violence and only words of love.
No more greed is what we need, both here on earth and up above.
And no more ego and what is 'mine', cause we've come up against the end of the line.
The weather's hot, can't say that it's not or we'll ride a sinking boat.
So no more talk of spirit and no more talk of soul.
Until we've taken up the mantle. Until we've reached our goal.
And then we can be so virtuous, like angels told of old.
And then we can be victorious. And raise the winner's gold.

Where are we going" What will we do? And who will make the change?
Will it be me or will it be you? How far will we extend the range?

May It Continue

May the brown earth and the green leaves
thrive in color and in grace.
May it continue.

May the clear air and the cumulocirrus clouds
be there in the sky and in each breath, always.
May it continue.

May the water made of sweet minerals and salt
in small streams and large rivers
flow forever and forever flow to the seas.
May it continue.

May the sun shine warm and bright
and the moon give light at night—shining from shook foil.
May it continue.

May the beautiful birds of Hawaii and
the luminous parrots of Peru fly far and fast
and may their number grow.
May it continue.

May the deer and the elk, the antelope and the ibis
move and migrate, leap and lope across plain
and wooded plateau.
May it continue.

May the whale and the dolphin and the manatee
swim deep in dark oceans and lagoons   and sing.
May it continue.

May the elephants forever in families roam,
trunk to tail, trumpeting bliss.
May it continue.

May waves of warm frost linger in bush and blaze
that puts fire in the peat of loam. And let lick cry from ripe vine.
May it continue.

May the rose climb through
the cold murmur of morning dirt.
May dark mulch coax tendrils from sleep.
May it continue.

May wild words come flying from green coils and
may each breath rustle through the beard of blue moss
in the sound of song.
May it continue.

Prayer for the Earth

The earth is my body, and I
shall not want;
It beckons me to lie down in green pastures.
It shares with me its clean waters, and
it nurtures my soul.
It leads me along the paths of right-thinking
for its own sake.

Even though I walk through
valleys among shadows of darkness,
I fear no evil, for the earth is with me;
its mountains and its seas,
they comfort me.

O great Earth, you have set a banquet before me
on the table of this Garden,
have filled my mind with revelations,
and my wonder grows!
Surely the deer and the seasons shall
follow me
all the days of my life;
and I will live in the beauty of
this world
forever.
E-man'u. Amen.

Image Index

Cover: Diamond Hill in County Galway, Connemara National Park, Ireland

Page: 1 Lunar Eclipse, Whittier, NC
Page 5: Barn Owl, Homosassa Springs, FL
Page 6: Castlerigg Stone Circle, Keswick, England
Page 8: Charlies Bunion, GSMNP
Page 10: Ginnie Springs, High Springs, Florida
Page 12: Waterfall near Blue Ridge Parkway, Western North Carolina
Page 14: Poarch Creek Pow Wow, Atmore, Alabama
Page 16: Long Meg and Her Daughters Stone Circle, Penrith, England
Page 18: Trail to Cliff Tops, Great Smoky Mountains National Park
Page 20: Sunrise through Fog, Kuwohi Mountain, Great Smoky Mountains National Park
Page 22: Water along Highway 441, Great Smoky Mountains National Park
Page 25: Gulf of Mexico Oil Spill Disaster of Oil on Sand, Gulf Shores, Alabama
Page 26: Bull Elk, Great Smoky Mountains National Park
Page 29: Creek in Great Smoky Mountains National Park
Page 31: Sunrise, Great Smoky Mountains National Park
Page 32: Kituwah—Cherokee Mother Town, Western North Carolina
Page 35: Riceville Valley Snowfall, Asheville, North Carolina
Page 36: Cousins—Gulf of Mexico, Orange Beach, Alabama
Page 37: The Abbey, Glastonbury, England
Page 38: Shooting Star, Great Smoky Mountains National Park
Page 40: New Growth, Great Smoky Mountains National Park
Page 43: Akumal, Mexico
Page 49: Triple Falls, Brevard, NC
Page 50: Spring growth with Snail, Great Smoky Mountains National Park
Page 54: Jack in the Pulpit, Great Smoky Mountains National Park
Page 56: Hoar Frost, Newfound Gap, Great Smoky Mountains National Park
Page 59: Dogwood Blossom, Great Smoky Mountains National Park
Page 61: Creek, Great Smoky Mountains National Park
Page 62: Star Trails, Whittier, North Carolina
Page 66: Raindrop, Magnolia Springs, Alabama
Page 68: Mingo Falls, Cherokee, North Carolina
Page 72: Thors Cave, Peak District National Park, UK
Page 74: Underwater Cave, Tulum, Mexico
Page 76: Hoh Rainforest, Olympic National Park, Forks, Washington
Page 78: Aurora, Kuwohi Mountain, Great Smoky Mountains National Park
Page 80: Alum Cave Trail, Great Smoky Mountains National Park

Page 83: Kuwohi Mountain, Great Smoky Mountains National Park
Page 84: Inis Mor, Ireland
Page 86: Dove Cottage, Grasmere, England
Page 88: Stairway to Heaven, Waterrock Knob, Blue Ridge Parkway
Page 90: Creek, Great Smoky Mountains National Park
Page 92: Mingus Mill, Great Smoky Mountains National Park
Page 94: Appalachian Trail, Newfound Gap, Great Smoky Mountains National Park
Page 96: Appalachian Trail at Kuwohi, Great Smoky Mountains National Park
Page 98: Humpback Whale, Atlantic Ocean
Page 100: Bull Elk, Great Smoky Mountains National Park
Page 102: Ginnie Springs at Sante Fe River, High Springs, Florida
Page 104: Juvenile Elk, Great Smoky Mountains National Park
Page 106: Lady Slippers, Great Smoky Mountains National Park

Thomas Rain Crowe is an internationally-published and recognized author, editor and translator of more than thirty books, including the multi-award winning nonfiction nature memoir *Zoro's Field: My Life in the Appalachian Woods (2005)*; *The End of Eden: Writings of an Environmental Activist* (2008); an internationally acclaimed anthology of contemporary Celtic language poets entitled *Writing the Wind: A Celtic Resurgence* (The New Celtic Poetry) and his collection of poetry *The Laugharne Poems* written at the Dylan Thomas boathouse in Laugharne, Wales in 1993 and 1995. He has translated two volumes of the Sufi poet Hafiz—*In Wineseller's Street* (Iran Books) and *Drunk On the Wine of the Beloved* (Shambhala Press). He has belonged to and worked with several environmental organizations, has been an editor of major literary and cultural journals and anthologies and is founder and publisher of New Native Press (www.newnativepress.org). He lived in San Francisco during the 1970s working alongside all the people cited in his most recent book *Starting From San Francisco: Beats, Baby Beats & The 1970s San Francisco Renaissance* and was an original member of the group responsible for the resurrection of *Beatitude* magazine during those years as well as working with various bioregional groups in northern California. He is a longtime resident of the Southern Appalachians and lives in the Tuckasegee watershed and the "Little Canada" community of Jackson County in western North Carolina, USA. His archives are collected and housed at the Special Collections Library at Duke University.

Simone Lipscomb has photographed nature for 47 years. She has been a creative writer since fourth grade where her imaginative stories earned a place on the teacher's A+++ wall.

She documented the BP Deepwater Horizon Gulf of Mexico Oil Spill for a year, choosing seven areas of public land to follow from before, during, and after the disaster.

Simone has photographed humpback whales, dolphins, sea lions, sea turtles, and other friends of the ocean. She has a deep love for wild places and wild life.

Several books of her photography and prose have been published. She has included children in her efforts of environmental education, with three of her eleven books produced especially for kids.

An active short-essay writer, Simone produces regular essays with her nature photographs. She also produces videos focused on nature and environmental education.

Simone is a musician playing piano, djembee, frame drums, native flutes, and Celtic whistles. She often pairs her music with videos she produces.

You can follow her on her website at: SimoneLipscomb.com and her YouTube channel @SimoneLipscomb.

She's an avid hiker in the Smoky Mountains, as well as a fly fisher. Simone always seeks the energetic connection to all life as a way to inform her path.

www.ingramcontent.com/pod-product-compliance
Lightning Source LLC
Chambersburg PA
CBHW040302170426
43193CB00021B/2978